THEOPHANY
{THE PRESENCE OF GOD}

LOIS TSCHIDA
&
GERMAINE SMITH

THE CENTER FOR HEALING PRESS

© 2016 by Lois Tschida and Germaine Smith.
All rights reserved.

Photographs by Lois Tschida.
Poetry by Germaine Smith.

ISBN : 978-0-9960421-1-6 (print)
Library of Congress Control Number: 2016906403

All rights reserved.
No portion of this publication may be reproduced or transmitted in any form or by any means, electronic or mechanical, including photocopying, recording, or capturing on any information storage and retrieval system, without permission in writing from the publisher, except by a reviewer who may quote brief passages in a critical article or review to be printed in a magazine or newspaper, or electronically transmitted on radio, television, or Internet.

For photograph reprint or sale information, contact Lois at: www.sharedspiritcards.com
or ldtschida@hotmail.com
For book reprint permission, email germ@thecenterforhealing.us.

The Center for Healing Press is the imprint of The Center for Healing.
Contact: germ@thecenterforhealing.us.

Front Cover picture: Lake Superior, Two Harbors, MN
Back Cover picture: Aquilegia Blue Columbine, Paul. MN.

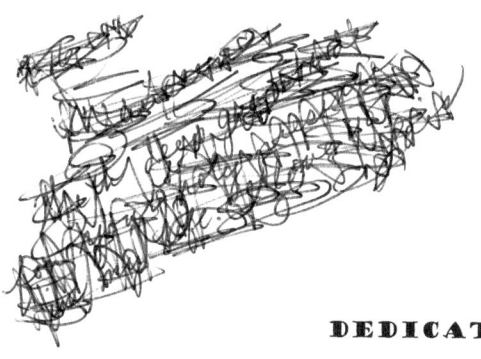

DEDICATIONS

Sr. Maureen Kelly, OSF
and
Fr. John Clay
(whom I love and consider
my spiritual parents)

Melissa Johnson
(for laughter in toxic times)
and
Lois Tschida
(for beauty in winter wastelands)

THANKSGIVINGS

Mary McPherson
(for clarity of vision)
and
Mary Mohan
(for searching and finding the answers)
and
Connor Blacksher
(for doing what I could not)

CONTENTS

A	Colorado River	Always	2
B	Lake Superior	Balance	4
C	Orange Roses	Celebration	6
D	Blue Crocuses	Discover	8
E	Milk Week	Essential	10
F	Minnehaha Falls	Fall	12
G	Colorado River	Grace	14
H	MN Arboretum	Harmony	16
I	Havasu Sunris	Invitation	18
J	Wild Yellow Rose	Jewel	20
K	Rink Sunset	Kindle	22
L	Dandelion	Limitless	24
M	Purple Clematis	Magic	26
N	Purple Iris	Noble	28
O	Lupines & Birch	One	30
P	Palo Verde Tree	Perspective	32
Q	Crabapple Tree	Quintessence	34
R	Casey Lake	Reflection	36
S	Red Coral Flower	Sweetness	38
T	Pansy	Tickle	40
U	Lake Havasu	Unabridged	42
V	Pine Cone	Vibrancy	44
W	Lake Michigan	Wild	46
X	Morning Glories	X	48
Y	Wild Columbine	Yield	50
Z	Sherburne Sunset	Zenith	52

INTRODUCTION

During a frightful night of intense loneliness,
I longed to hear God's voice
telling me that I belonged and was loved.

That was the inspiration for writing this book
of God's messages to me—
what I hoped the Divine would say
if only I could hear.

As the idea developed
I thought of my friend Lois
and her stunning photography.
Not only wanting to hear a message
from the Divine
I needed to open my eyes
to the beauty of God
manifested throughout all creation.

Hence "Theophany".
The photographs demonstrate
the Presence of God in nature.
The poetry,
written from the Divine's point of view,
indicates what I hope
we all might be open to hearing.

A

Colorado River meets Lake Havasu

Lake Havasu City, AZ

February 2008

"A" is Always.

What do I need to say to you?
Or rather,
    what do you need to hear from Me?

Will you hear Me if I tell you
    you are invaluable...
    full of dignity?

Because I am with you,
    will you embrace your fearlessness
        as well as your responsibility?

Since you and I are united,
    will you trust in My Guidance
        and give Me your confidence?

Are you willing to see, hear, feel, know
    My Theophany—
    My Presence—
        everywhere?

Will you be open to the reality that with Me
    you will never know complete defeat...
    you will experience complete peace?

B
Lake Superior

Two Harbors, MN

July 2013

"B" is Balance.

You are the perfect balance
of body and soul
of Earth and Divinity

of tenderness and tenacity
of compassion and courage
of patience and persistence

of unfolding Beauty
of knowing Mystery.

C
Orange Roses
Maplewood, MN[1]
June 2011

---
[1] Roses from my doctoral graduation party

"C" is Celebration.

I celebrate you.

I celebrate your transformation
    from lost soul to wise sage.
You have overcome the barren and inert soil
    to stretch to the light.

I celebrate your thorns,
    sharp defensive barbs that sought
    not aggression but self-protection.

I celebrate your velvet soft petals,
    tenderness that belies great power.
Though appearing quite fragile,
    you withstand the fiercest storms.

I celebrate your unfolding,
    your opening, listening to love's prompts
    your coming into full bloom.

I celebrate you.
Will you celebrate with Me?

D

Blue-purple Crocus

St. Paul, MN[2]

April 2011

---

[2]From the garden of Sr. Maureen Kelly, OSF.

"D" is Discover.

Deep within you,
lies a fertile ground
of possibility,
waiting to shed winter's coat
and be born.

I see your radiance
hidden beneath and
eagerly await its return.

Break through
the crust of doubt
to discover
your brilliance.

E

Milk Weed

Frontenac, MN

September 2012

"E" is Essential.

Milk weed is not a weed at all.
It is an essential part of the cosmos!

As a perennial, it thrives with strong roots
    living through harsh Minnesota winters.
As these roots are used medicinally,
    their scientific name, Asclepias,
        is that of the Greek god of medicine.[3]
The leaves of the milkweed are vital also—
    the only food source
        for the monarch butterfly.
Hence, despite its name, milk weed is essential.

As are you.
Your strong roots ground you
    in harsh climates.
Within you is the power to be a medicine
    to heal the wounds
        of yourself and others.
You are a beacon of refreshment and
    nourishment to all who come to you.

You, like the milk weed,
    are an essential part of the cosmos!

---

[3] http://wildblessing.com/plants/milkweed/ (12/25/16)

F

Minnehaha Falls

Minneapolis, MN

July 2014

"F" is Fall.

You are not falling down or falling over
	or falling to pieces or falling apart.

You are falling into Me.

Let go of your footing, your grip,
	your dreams, your control,
	your security, your hope—
		fall into Me.

Fall into the space that is Me
	and land on the ground that is Me.

And on the way down,
	trust Me
	and
	enjoy.

G
Colorado River meets Lake Havasu
Lake Havasu City, AZ
January 2009

"G" is Grace.

I have waited for you to turn to Me.
And waited...
And waited...
Patiently....
Anticipating....

And then it happened: you turned to Me.
We touched.
And in that moment, fulfilled My name—
Grace.

H
MN Landscape Arboretum
Chaska, MN
May 2011

"H" is Harmonious.

Why do you insist on fighting yourself?
Do you not know all of you
      is embraced by Me?

See how the colors and kinds of nature
      exist together.
They share space,
      take only what they need,
      receive what Earth gives,
      fulfill their undertaking,
      bloom in season.

Harmonious they are
      in the accepting of their dignity
      and
      in the embracing of My esteem.

I

Sunrise

Lake Havasu City, AZ

January 2012

"I" is Invitation.

Each day the earth turns
    to invite Me to illuminate her.
Restorative Light erases darkness.
Brilliance sparkles everywhere.

Gloom's hold is broken.
Light penetrates
    the horizon's every crevice.
All at the earth's bidding.

Each day the earth turns,
      asks,
         and I respond.

Will you turn to Me?
Invite Me in for a day of Light?

J
Wild Yellow Rose
St. Paul, MN
June 2011

"J" is Jewel.

Such a beautiful jewel!
Such an exquisitely beautiful, unfolding jewel!

Will you come into My garden,
     I want my roses to meet you.[4]

---

[4]Richard Brinsley, http://www.brainyquote.com/quotes/quotes/richardbri161822.html (2/15/16).

K

Hockey Rink

Minneapolis, MN

January 2005

"K" is Kindle.

Kindle a fire of passion...
    a fire of love.

Kindle a breath of refreshment...
    a breath of tranquility.

Kindle an enthusiasm for optimism...
    an enthusiasm for hopefulness.

Kindle an embrace of acceptance...
    an embrace of forgiveness.

Kindle fervor for integrity...
    a fervor for truth.

Kindle a passion for service...
    a passion for gratitude.

L

Dandelion

North Shore of Lake Superior, MN

July 2014

"L" is Limitless.

You conceive of one solution; I multiple.
You escape by running away; I stand firm.

You feel the wounds; I the wholeness.
You perceive the complexity; I the simplicity.

You see the dying; I the transformation.
You sense the defeat; I the victory.

You fear the end in death;
    I welcome the beginning.
You believe in one path to Me;
    I know all paths lead to Me.

M
Purple Clematis

St. Paul, MN

June 2014

"M" is Magic.

All creation dances with magic:
the magic of creativity
fashioning art from ashes,

the magic of love
uniting intimacy with vulnerability,

the magic of laughter
weaving humor and humility,

the magic of recovery
building grace upon brokenness.

Look!
Magic is there...
And there...
And there....

N
Purple Iris

St. Paul, MN

May 2012

""N" is Noble.

Gracious Elegant Compassionate
are you.

Unblemished Dignified Grand
are you.

Principled Gallant Heroic
are you.

Noble
are you.

O

Wild Lupines with Birch

Two Harbors, MN

July 2011

"O" is One.

I am with you because I am in you.
You and I were born at the same time.[5]

There is no place you go that I cannot reach,
      no distance I cannot close.
Whether the bottom of a brandy bottle
      or the disease of busyness
      or the black hole of depression
      or the heights of ego
      I am with you.

You may seek to run from Me
      but you cannot out run yourself.
When you fear Me,
      you really fear yourself.

Where you go, I am already there.
You and I are One.

---

[5] Richard Hooper, ed., The Essential Mystics, Poets, Saints, and Sages, (Charlottesville, VI ,Hampton Road, Publishing, 2013), 109.

P

Blue Palo Verde Tree
Lake Havasu City, AZ
February 2007

"P" is Perspective.

What you see as barren, I know as rich.
What you feel is infertile, I experience as full.

When you sense no growth,
    I see gestation.
When you fear stagnation,
    I perceive possibility.

I see deepest roots, not empty branches,
    aged toughness, not parched bark..

Our perspectives are different.
Yours is limited, finite, particular,
    and often self-serving.
I see boundless potential
    completing the intentional purpose.

Though you see naught, I see your path.

Q

Flowering Crabapple Tree

St. Paul, MN

April 2010

"Q" is Quintessence

Why do you insist upon
    trying to be like everybody else?

Your DNA is programmed for authenticity
    not conformity.
Your individuality shouts brilliance
    not mediocrity.
Your character's rooted in integrity
    not popularity.
Your worth and dignity are birthrights,
    not based on imaginary rankings
        of others.

Throw off the comfort of conformity
    and bask in your own identity.
Your quintessence, your core essence,
    longs to dance in the garden of life.
Be fearless in being you.

R

Casey Lake

North St. Paul, MN

May 2005

"R" is Reflection.

When I look in the mirror, I see you.

I see your beauty—
      skin and soul aged exquisitely
      through tough lessons.

I see your power—
      confidence and determination
      from a bottomless well of reserve.

I see your vulnerability—
      Hesitatingly tender openness
      covered with scars.

When I look in the mirror, I see you.
Who do you see when you look in the mirror?

S

Red Coral Flower

St. Paul, MN

August 2012

"S" is Sweetness.

Drink deeply from the well of sweetness.
Life is not meant to be drudgery
    but a celebration.

Look back.
See how far you have come—
    the trials you have conquered,
    the lessons you have learned.

Gulp the casks of hope.
Sip the nectar of anticipation.
Savor the bouquet of accomplishment.

There will be more trials to overcome,
    more mountains to climb.

So today—for today—
    drink deeply from the well of sweetness.

T

Pansy

St. Maplewood, MN

May 2012

"T" is Tickle.

Come play with Me
in my cathedral called nature.

The trees are longing for a companion;
the flowers wish a playmate;
the waters want to splash you with delight.

Too much worry has dampened your view
until all you feel is hard labor.

You need refreshment
in My garden of sweet joy
where velvet petals of tranquility fill you.

Come play with Me and dance in the colors.
Tickle Me with your laughter.

U

Lake Havasu

Lake Havasu City, AZ

January 2005

"U" is Unabridged.

I AM not condensed
    not reduced
    not shortened.

I AM complete
    full
    comprehensive
    infinite
    universal.

There is no place you will find Me unfinished
    or partial or finite.

Just look....
I AM unabridged everywhere
    and unabridged in everything.

V

Flowering Pine Cone

St. Paul, MN

May 2012

"V" is Vibrancy.

Come outside.
Spending too many minutes and decades
    hiding inside your walls leaves you
    contained and captured,
    bound, and beige.

Inside the walls, existence is
    regulated and controlled and structured
        mediocrity devoid of
        authentic freedom;
    taupe and tan and khaki and cream
    a dullness absent the vibrancy of color.

Come outside and sink into the soil of delight.
Unfettered, let the wind and water and aroma
    delight your every cell.

Freed,
    bedazzled by colors
    exploding with radiance!

Come outside and play with Life.

W

Lake Michigan
Ludington, MI
August 2011

"W" is Wild.

There's something wild within you!
Untamed
Unexplored
Unbroken
Cavernous
Fresh

It is spirit, not of bitterness, but boldness
Not vicious,
but veracity, uncontained and uncontainable.

Wild as in the passionate bursting forth
of energy and matter joined
in a mission of being!

Let it roll
bubbling up and over itself
in eager anticipation of exposure.

Let it roar
as the explosion of the waves
crashing against the shore.

Let it rise
the Wild Divine and Wild Earth within you.

X

Morning Glories
Frontenac, MN
September 2011

"X" is X.[6]

I AM.
I AM beyond labels,
    limitless and unbounded.
No name or description can contain Me.

I AM everywhere, revealed in everything.
Nothing has its being without My prompting.

I AM seen in the epiphany—
    of love that kindles hearts
    color that dazzles all creation
    species beyond all counting.

I AM unseen in the transformation—
    hearts wounded and weeping
    seeds broken then blooming
    humans' unconscious
        finding awakening.

I am unknown,
    beyond human understanding
    yet within human reach.
I AM Source and Destination.

---

[6]"X" denotes the symbol for the unknown quantity in mathematical equations. http://gizmodo.com/why-we-use-x-as-the-unknown-in-math-1657254357 (3/23/16).

Y

Wild Columbine

Collegeville, MN

May 2012

"Y" is Yield.

Yield to yield.
Yield to Me your defects.
Surrender your arrogance, bitterness, greed,
    self-righteousness, sense of entitlement, resentments, mean-spiritedness, mistrust, self-pity, playing the victim.

Yield to Me your strengths.
Surrender your gentleness, openness, willingness, empathy, forgiving nature,
    sense of responsibility, determination,
    power, honesty, dedication, wisdom.

Yield to Me all of you
    and you will yield a new you.
You will be a garden of peace—
    rooted in My strength,
    blossoming with My passion.

Yield to yield.

Z

Sherburne National Wildlife Refuge

Zimmerman, MN

July 2011

"Z" is Zenith.

I AM Zenith,
the highest point.

I AM
relentless Truth
ruthless Compassion
penetrating Light
creative Darkness
satisfied Yearning
broken Wholeness
permeating Bliss.

I AM
longing Culmination
ultimate Destination

I AM
Home.